editing made easy

For

Haya Kaplan

Nachum Kaplan

and

Suzie Cox

Upper Access books may be purchased in quantity at substantial discounts by book clubs, writers' groups, schools, businesses, and other organizations. If you have use for 10 or more copies of this book, or any other Upper Access title, please contact us for details. We can be reached at 802-482-2988 or *info@upperaccess.com*.

Bruce Kaplan

editing made easy
simple rules for effective writing

Upper Access, Inc., Book Publishers
87 Upper Access Road
Hinesburg, Vermont 05461
www.upperaccess.com

Upper Access, Inc., Book Publishers
87 Upper Access Road
Hinesburg, VT 05461

Cover design and interior layout by Kitty Werner, RSBPress, Waitsfield, Vermont

Cover photo of computer © iStockphoto.com/Kaczka

This edition of *Editing Made Easy* is created for distribution in the United States of America. Some of its contents have been published in different form by Bruce Kaplan, © 1999 and 2010, and by Penguin Books Australia Ltd., © 2003.

ISBN 978-0-942679-36-6 (trade paper)

ISBN 978-0-942679-38-0 (electronic)

Library of Congress Cataloging-in-Publication Data

Kaplan, Bruce, 1942-
   Editing made easy : simple rules for effective writing / Bruce Kaplan.
      p. cm.
   Includes index.
   ISBN 978-0-942679-36-6 (trade paper : alk. paper)
   1. Editing. 2. English language--Rhetoric. I. Title.
   PN162.K26 2012
   808.02'7--dc23   2012003412

Printed in the United States of America

12 / 10 9 8 7 6 5 4 3 2 1

about the author

Bruce Kaplan is a newspaper copy editor and editorial trainer with international experience spanning more than 40 years. He has held senior positions with major publications in Australia, Hong Kong and Singapore. He trains editors and writers for newspapers and magazines, and tutors at writers' centers and tertiary education institutions. He may be reached at *editeasy@hotmail.com*.

praise for international editions of this book

"Finally, a book about editing and writing concisely that is actually written —concisely. Too many books about editing suffer from exactly the sort of problems they profess to solve: dense, difficult copy that is almost impossible to penetrate. But this book lays it out simply and in a matter-of-fact style. As a long-time journalist and editor, it now occupies an important place on my bookshelf—right next to me. Anyone else interested in the craft of words will reserve the same place for it."

—Gary Linnell, national editor, *Fairfax Media*, Australia

"Part of a writer's job is to make it easy for an editor to say yes. Bruce Kaplan's *Editing Made Easy* helps achieve this. It should be on every writer's bookshelf next to *Elements of Style* and *Modern English Usage*."

—Barry Watts, tutor in professional writing and editing, Centre for Adult Education, Melbourne, Australia

"Clear, concise and appealing like the writing it promotes. *Editing Made Easy* is an invaluable guide for the beginner and an essential memory-jog for the experienced journalist."

—Colin McKinnon, training editor, *The Age*, Melbourne, Australia

"*Editing Made Easy* has been one of my bibles in training English language journalists in Malaysia and Bangladesh."

—Pieter Wessels, trainer, Commonwealth Journalists Association, United Kingdom

"This book gets right to the point. There is no excess here. Reading Bruce Kaplan, one sometimes feels like a light has been turned on or the mists have cleared on many topics."

—AuthorsDen, United States of America

"I teach magazine journalism to approximately 60 students across the year. *Editing Made Easy* is clear, concise and accessible for trainees."

—Sheridan McCoid, lecturer, Brighton Center for Journalism, United Kingdom

"This energetic book is an indispensable tool for writers, journalists, advertising professionals, universities and anyone desiring an easy-to-use editing guide."

—*Writing Queensland* magazine, Queensland Writers Centre, Australia

contents

author's note

This book is a revised and expanded version of my original book, *Editing Made Easy*, first published in Australia in 1999. I have added chapters, and enlarged some previously published chapters, with more examples and more comprehensive explanations. Significantly, this edition accommodates the rules, conventions, and spellings of American English.

This book is non-technical. My aim is to provide straightforward, practical guidelines for editing, not discuss advanced English grammar. So, although I refer when necessary to such basic terms as *noun, verb* and *pronoun,* you will find no loftier technical grammatical terms here, such as *present perfect progressive, correlative conjunctions, imperative mood* or *interrogative adjective.*

However, a note of caution is in order. Much of the advice in this book is not to be written in stone. English is a flexible language, and writing a creative calling. There are many acceptable ways for writers to express themselves.

For example, I make the point that two or three short sentences are often better than one long sentence. This is certainly true—but it does not mean there is no room for a well-crafted longer sentence that expresses something important in a certain way or adds to the lyricism, rhythm or power of a text.

Likewise, I warn against using too much passive voice because it can slow the pace. But there are sometimes occasions when the passive voice is needed to maintain a cohesive, flowing narrative.

So be flexible. The purpose of this book is to put the odds on your side; to increase your chances of being published or finding success as a reporter, feature writer, novelist, freelance writer, blogger, Web developer, Web editor, communications consultant, advertising copywriter, speechwriter or public relations consultant—in fact anything involving the written word.

Bruce Kaplan, 2012

why learn editing?
the benefits for you

So why learn how to edit? Most importantly, learning to edit will make you a more proficient, more polished writer. It will improve your writing in more ways than you might ever imagine. It will do the same for people whose writing you edit.

This book will give you the practical skills and techniques that professional editors use every day. The advice applies to almost all forms of writing. Exceptions may occur with fiction, scientific and academic writing, and personal expressions such as e-mail and Facebook. But most of the rules apply across the board.

Essentially, this book is about plain English. The advice will help you add punch and clarity to reports, feature articles, press releases, hard news, newsletters, brochures, business communications, short stories, staff bulletins, business proposals, non-fiction books and—yes—even novels.

Writing is a demanding, exacting, rewarding and enriching craft. Proficiency in editing is the key to excellence in writing.

lean and clean

what editors do

A skilled writer or editor's goal is to get the message across clearly and accurately. Whatever you are writing, the minute it becomes long-winded, garbled, confusing or boring, communication has broken down. Clear, active, interesting English is the key to skilled writing and editing.

Keep your writing and editing lean and clean.

Of course, there are a few secrets. The professionals know them, because that is their job. But there are no tricks. There is no mystique, no magic formula. It is a matter of knowing the rules and the conventions.

The aim is simplicity—how to write and edit text so everyone can understand what the writer wants to say. Learn to do this and you are on your way to becoming a competent and effective writer and editor.

But first, let us clear up an area of common confusion about the meaning of the word *editor*. In the magazine and newspaper world, the word *editor* appears in many forms—editor, copy editor, sub-editor, chief sub-editor, chief copy editor, news editor, night editor, day editor, features editor, city editor, layout editor. These titles refer to various areas of responsibility and hierarchy.

Often the editor of a major newspaper does no editing at all, which comes as something of a surprise to many people. The editor of a major newspaper carries a huge responsibility. He or she is responsible for the publication as a whole and for everything that appears in the paper.

The terms *copy editor* and *sub-editor* mean the same thing. *Copy* refers to any written text. Whether it is a news report or a feature story, *editors* edit *copy*. *Copy editor* is the American term and *sub-editor* is the English term. However, *copy editor* is slowly becoming more common worldwide. Throughout this book I use the word *editor* to mean copy editor or sub-editor.

So what does a professional editor do? A brainstorming session might come up with the following editorial tasks. An editor should:

- check spelling

- check punctuation

- check grammar

- check facts

- check names—of people, companies, organizations, streets, cities, suburbs, countries and sports teams

- turn long, unwieldy sentences into short, clear sentences

- turn long paragraphs into short paragraphs

- keep copy in the active voice when possible

- eliminate unnecessary words

- turn long words into short words

- when appropriate turn nouns into verbs to make the writing more active

- write captions for photographs

- write headlines

- make sure copy meets legal requirements and is not defamatory

- cut copy to length, according to layout and design requirements

- ensure everything can be easily understood and nothing can be misunderstood.

Quite a list, isn't it? If we summarize an editor's responsibilities, we see that editors have three main tasks:

1. To ensure copy is written in the best possible way using plain English.

2. To check everything for accuracy and legality.

3. To ensure copy meets technical requirements—for example, to fit stories and headlines into the space allowed.

So switch on your computers and pick up your pens. We are on our way.

the golden rules
for professional writing and editing

These 12 golden rules are your first step toward becoming a skilled editor. Learn them and never forget them. They are the key to your success.

1. Write and edit to express, not to impress.

2. Always write/edit so everything can be easily understood.

3. Always write/edit so that nothing can be misunderstood.

4. Say what you mean, clearly and simply.

5. Use short sentences.

6. Use short paragraphs.

7. Use the simplest words possible.

8. Write in the active voice.

9. Avoid unnecessary words.

10. Use verbs for action.

11. Avoid clichés and jargon.

12. If in doubt, leave it out.

ruthless people
what makes a good editor?

So, what is the secret to good copy editing?

Well, no item escapes the eye of the skilled editor. She or he will home in on a misplaced comma, a split infinitive, a misused word or an error of fact. The skilled editor pays ruthless attention to detail.

Such attention to detail can mean the difference between your writing being understood or misunderstood, accepted for publication or rejected. It can mean the difference between a reader finishing an article or becoming bored.

So you must be a tough editor of all text, including your own.

Be mean to yourself to be kind to yourself. Check, check and check again that your basic ingredients are correct. Check grammar, spelling, punctuation and facts.

Have you spelled the names of people correctly and consistently throughout? Never assume you know how to spell a name. Is it *Shuman, Shumann, Schuman or Schumann*?

Have you spelled street, road and place names correctly? Are you sure you have not written *Carribean* (wrong) instead of *Caribbean* (right) or *Phillipines* (wrong) instead of *Philippines* (right)?

When writing hard news, have you remembered to include such details as people's ages and where they live or come from? Have you been clear about attribution? Is it clear who is saying what and to whom? Have you checked that what you have written is not libelous and that any controversial claims are substantiated? If you cannot prove something or are unsure about it, delete it. Remember, *if in doubt, leave it out.*

Naturally, an editor cannot know everything, so he or she has tools on hand to help. Sometimes a quick internet search will suffice. But free online resources can be incomplete and unreliable. We still need good dictionaries, style books and other authoritative reference works published on paper or electronically. Remember—*check, check and check again.*

be active
avoiding the passive voice

One little word should set an editor's mental alarm bells ringing:

by

This word, which we use in speech every day, often tells us we are writing in the passive voice not the active. In writing and editing, using the passive voice is often problematic, as you will see.

"But why?" I hear you cry. "What is wrong with such a cute little word? I use it all the time, certainly when I speak and often when I write."

Well, forget about how you talk. How we speak and how we write are different. In writing, this inoffensive little word *by*, unless used appropriately, can turn an interesting sentence into a boring one.

Certainly, the word *by* can be used in some contexts that are not the passive voice. There is no problem with use of the word in the following sentences:

I will be gone by the time you get here.

Or:

Shall we meet down by the river?

Our concern in this section is to give a sentence more immediacy, a stronger sense of action, of something happening. For that we need the active voice

So, what is the difference between the *active* voice and the *passive* voice? And what is the meaning of *voice*, anyway? Well, there is no mystery. *Voice* is the characteristic of a *verb* (a doing word) that tells us whether the subject of the verb is performing the action of the verb (*active voice*) or whether the subject is acted upon (*passive voice*).

Consider this sentence:

> *Three people were chased in a city park by a man with a stick yesterday.*

This is the passive voice. The fact that the sentence contains the word *by* tells you so. The subject *(three people)* is acted upon *(by a man with a stick).*

> *A man with a stick chased three people in a city park yesterday.*

This is the active voice. When we us the active voice, notice the difference.

Some other basic examples:

> **Passive:** *The report was finished on time by me.*

> **Active:** *I finished the report on time.*

> **Passive:** *The books were carried home by me.*

> **Active:** *I carried the books home.*

> **Passive:** *I was bored to death by the speaker.*

> **Active:** *The speaker bored me to death.*

There are ways in which the passive voice can be used to add balance and flow, depending on context. For example:

A student wrote the first essay, the second essay was written by an office worker, and a pensioner wrote the third one.

Or the passive voice might be appropriate depending on the most important point of a sentence. For example:

Passive: *My computer was stolen by a burglar last night.*

Active: *A burglar stole my computer last night.*

However, if the point is really that the computer has been stolen, not who stole it, we could write in the passive:

My computer was stolen last night.

But if you knew who stole your computer, you would then write in the active:

My idiot roommate stole my computer last night.

We might also use the passive voice in this next example:

Passive: *The broken power lines were fixed by workers last night.*

Active: *Workers fixed the broken power lines last night.*

However, this is an example of where another form of passive voice—which does not even use the word *by*—might be appropriate, because who else would be fixing the power lines but workers? So it would be acceptable to write:

The broken power lines were fixed last night.

Another example of this would be:

Passive: *The hearing was adjourned by the judge.*

Active: *The judge adjourned the hearing.*

Again, in this case the passive voice might also be acceptable:

The hearing was adjourned until Friday.

After all, who but the judge would adjourn the case?

If you count the words in many of these examples, you will see that sentences in the active voice generally contain fewer words. This is a another reason for writing in the active voice. Brevity is a secret of good writing and editing. Do not waste words. Keep things "tight," where every word means something.

Imagine you are a professional writer and you have to produce a story of a certain length. Writing in the active voice will make it much easier for you to tell your story in the required 2000 words, rather than 2200.

Editors need to know how to save words. Too much passive voice tends to slow the text, turning a potentially interesting story or report into a pedestrian plod.

A good idea is to write in the active voice first. If you then feel the passive voice conveys the meaning or mood better in a particular sentence, use your discretion.

But remember, write in the active voice when possible and say goodbye to *by.*

split personalities
beware the split infinitive

Welcome to the controversial world of the split infinitive. Veteran editors on the receiving end of split infinitives can sometimes be seen waving their arms, shouting or sobbing at their desks. These guardians of language purity are the true believers in the grammar crime of the split infinitive.

But wait—another school of thought holds that there is nothing wrong with splitting the infinitive. Supporters of this school point out, with some justification, that there are times when the pure infinitive makes a sentence clumsy.

Before we deal with that, we must understand what an infinitive is. In grammatical terms, the word *infinitive* applies to *verbs*. Verbs, of course, are *doing* words—for example, *run, jump, eat, sleep*. The infinitive form of a verb includes *to*—for example, *to run, to jump, to eat, to sleep*.

We split the infinitive when we put an *adverb* (a word that tells us *how* the action was done) after the *to* and before the *verb*. It is easy to recognize an *adverb*, because these words almost always end in *ly*—swift*ly*, brave*ly*, peaceful*ly*, rude*ly*.

Here are some examples of split infinitives:

to quickly eat

to slowly turn

to quietly speak

to loudly argue

to restlessly sleep

to cunningly plan

to sadly remember

If we follow the strict grammatical rules, these should read:

to eat quickly

to turn slowly

to speak quietly

to argue loudly

to sleep restlessly

to plan cunningly

to remember sadly

Sometimes, depending on the sentence or phrase structure, the adverb sounds better before the *to*, or even at the beginning or end of the sentence. Take, for example, the following sentence with a split infinitive:

The teacher failed to properly explain the theory.

The split infinitive is *to properly explain.* The recommended grammar would be:

*The teacher failed to explain the theory **properly**.*

Supporters of the split infinitive (or those who are not fussed about it) also might well say that:

To really understand *(split infinitive) what happened, we must look at . . .*

sounds better than:

> *To understand really (pure infinitive) what happened,
> we must look at* . . .

or:

> *Really to understand (pure infinitive) what happened,
> we must look at* . . .

Enemies of the pure infinitive also believe split infinitives sometimes add emphasis, for example, in the *Star Trek* introduction:

> *to boldly go*

Does this pack more punch than *to go boldly?* You be the judge.

Those who do not mind split infinitives also point out that the taboo on using anything but the pure infinitive is an archaic rule based on Latin, in which it is impossible to split the infinitive.

But to argue that we should not worry about the split infinitive because the taboo comes from Latin is to argue that we should throw out many basic rules of English grammar.

In your own interests, when writing or editing your own or someone else's work—whether it is a short story or an article for a newspaper or a magazine—it is usually best to stick to the rules and not to split the infinitive.

Write each sentence *without* splitting infinitives. But if it looks unacceptably awkward, do not hesitate to change it. As long as you know the rule, you will know when to break it.

time for action
turning nouns into verbs

A **noun** is a *naming* word. Broadly speaking there are three kinds of noun:

1. **Proper nouns**—for special names (or *proper* names) that we give to people, pets, countries, ships, mountains and so on. *Bill, Fred, Lucy, Fluffy, Rover, Singapore, Taiwan* and *Mexico* are *proper nouns.*

2. **Common nouns**—any nouns that are not proper nouns. *House, car, plumber, writer, journalist, dog, mountain, cat, carpenter, computer, table, chair* and *book* are *common nouns.* Common nouns that express an intangible idea are known as *abstract nouns.* Words such as *announcement, provision, introduction, recognition, consideration, consolidation* and *exploration* are *abstract nouns.*

3. **Collective nouns**—for groups of like things, people or animals. A *herd* of cows, a *flock* of sheep, a *school* of fish, an *orchestra* and a *team* are *collective nouns.* You will learn more about collective nouns later in this book.

Verbs are *doing* words. There are many kinds of verbs, depending on the tense or how they are used. But a verb is always a doing word. Doing means action. *To run, to jump, to edit, to think, to wish,* he *wondered,* she *slept* and he *listened* are *verbs.*

The problem is that many writers often use an abstract noun instead of a verb. This slows the copy, often making it boring.

Verbs add action and interest, giving copy more punch. When possible, use a verb instead of a noun to bring a sentence to life. This will help you save words, too.

Consider this:

> *The council will allow for the provision of more funds for new roads.*

The sentence is clumsy and slow. Instead try:

> *The council will provide more money for new roads.*

When we use *will provide* (verb) instead of *the provision of* (noun) and delete a*llow for*, the sentence becomes shorter, more active and easier to read. Or consider this:

> *City banks are considering the introduction of new fees.*

Instead try:

> *City banks may introduce new fees.*

The verb *may introduce* is far more active and interesting than the noun *the introduction of*. Another example:

> *The factory will begin production of more engines next week.*

Instead try:

> *The factory will produce more engines beginning next week.*

Again, the sentence is more lively when we use *produce* (verb) instead of *production of* (noun).

Another example:

> *The army will begin the mobilization of all troops tomorrow.*

Instead try:

> *The army will begin mobilizing all troops tomorrow.*

When we use *begin mobilizing* (verb) instead of *the mobilization of* (noun), the sentence is direct and more urgent.

Or:

> *The teacher said the substitution of verbs for nouns was an important part of editing.*

Instead try:

> *The teacher said using verbs instead of nouns was an important part of editing.*

In this case, not only have we eliminated the noun (*the substitution of*), we have replaced it with a shorter verb (*using*). This makes the sentence even easier to read.

Sometimes, when we replace a noun with a verb, we need to switch the sentence around. For example:

> *He was waiting for approval of the plans.*

becomes:

> *He was waiting for the plans to be approved.*

In this case, the noun (*approval*) that was in the middle of the sentence has become the verb (*to be approved*) at the end of the sentence.

Or:

> *She said simplification of English was most important.*

It is better to write:

She said it was most important to simplify English.

We have made the sentence simpler and more immediate by replacing *simplification of* (noun) with *to simplify* (verb).

If you count the words in the examples, you will find that the sentences with verbs are usually shorter. Getting rid of unnecessary words is an important part of an editor's job. But even when words are not being saved, the sentences are easier to read and more interesting.

A word of warning: Do not turn nouns into nonsensical *fake verbs*. Consider the following incorrect sentence:

I copy-edited the article.

Copy (as used in this sentence) is not a verb. *Edit* is the verb. Therefore, the sentence should read:

I edited the copy.

Or:

I edited the article.

In recent years, "verbing" has become a trend among careless writers. Sometimes, the new verbs become widely accepted—after the first several million people became "friended" on Facebook, we have accepted "friend" as a verb in that specific context.

But in general, "verbing" grates on most readers and certainly most editors. Skilled writers and editors do not use made-up verbs such as *tasking, impacting, gifting, trending, RVing, FTPing, securitizing,* or *dialoging.*

small and pesky

two words that slow the pace

With few exceptions, the words *of the* are not needed. A useful technique is to take an adjectival or possessive approach to the nouns. We save words and it is easier to read. Consider this:

the manager of the bank

is:

the bank manager

the president of the company

is:

the company president

the cover of the book

is:

the book cover

the owner of the horse

is:

the horse's owner

the leader of the band

is:

the band leader

the captain of the team

is:

the team captain

the wheels of the bicycle

are:

the bicycle wheels

Here are examples of another type of sentence in which the words *of the* can be eliminated:

one of the protesters at the site

is:

one protester at the site

The word *one* already indicates that more than one protester is at the site. If there was only one protester, we would say *the protester*.
Other examples:

one of the women in the shop
one woman in the shop

one of the musicians in the orchestra
one musician in the orchestra

one of the chocolates fell out of the bag
a chocolate fell out of the bag

nuisance value
more overused words

Three more words to watch out for are *others, both* and *new*. In certain circumstances, these words are tautological. You need to think carefully about whether they are superfluous.

Others:

> *A three-car crash killed two people and seriously injured four others in Indianapolis yesterday.*

The word *others* is not needed. If the crash killed the other four, the sentence would begin: *A three-car crash killed six people.* The fact that they were injured tells us they were other people. What else could they be? Better to write:

> *A three-car crash killed two people and seriously injured four in Indianapolis yesterday.*

Another example:

> *A spokesman said police had caught three escapees, but that four others were still at large.*

Again, the word *others* is superfluous. We know the escapees the police did not catch are others. If police had caught all of the escapees, the sentence would say that police had caught all seven escapees. Better to write:

> *A spokesman said police had caught three escapees, but four were still at large.*

Both:

> *Both Christine Jones and Judith Smith said they had worked for two years to raise money for their trip.*

We do not need the word *both* here because we have named the women—we know we are talking about *both* women. It is better to write:

> *Christine Jones and Judith Smith said they had worked hard for two years to raise money for their trip.*

Another example:

> *Company president Felix Drevin resigned yesterday after profit slumped. His deputy, Kevin Meeth, said he would be staying "for the time being." But both Mr. Drevin and Mr. Meeth agreed it would take a miracle to save the company from bankruptcy.*

Because the third sentence names Mr. Drevin and Mr. Meeth, we do not need the word *both*. Better to write:

> *But Mr. Drevin and Mr. Meeth agreed it would take a miracle to save the company from bankruptcy.*

However, we could use the word *both* if the names were missing.

> *But both* agreed it would take a miracle to save the company from bankruptcy.

New:

> *A police spokesman said there had been no new developments.*

Well, any developments would be new, wouldn't they? So all that needs to be said is *no developments*.

Another example:

House prices are expected to fall at least 10 percent this year, a new survey shows.

Well, of course it's a new survey—otherwise it is unlikely we would be reporting it. All that needs to be said is *a survey shows*. We might state in the second or third sentence that the survey of nearly 2000 real estate agents was carried out this month and released yesterday.

Finally, never use that old tautology *set a new record*. A record, by its very nature, must be new. You can set a third record or another record—but not *a new* one.

So, think twice before writing *new survey, new report, new figures, new developments* or such-like. Usually the word *new* is not needed.

is that so?
how to avoid that

Another word we can often do without is *that*. Like *of the*, it slows the pace. Consider this:

>   *He said that he would return tomorrow.*

Instead try:

>   *He said he would return tomorrow.*

Or:

>   *She said that she had no plans to travel overseas.*

Instead try:

>   *She said she had no plans to travel overseas.*

Or:

>   *He said that he would finish his homework after supper.*

Better to write:

>   *He said he would finish his homework after supper.*

Or:

>   *They promised that they would be home before midnight.*

Better to write:

>   *They promised they would be home before midnight.*

A good idea is test the sentence out loud. Your ear will often confirm whether the word *that* is needed.

A word of warning. The word *that* can be used in many other ways. For example:

> *That is not the way to do it.*

Or:

> *Is that what you really mean?*

In these examples, *that* is clearly not superfluous.

every which way
the difference between which and that

Misuse of *which* when we mean *that* is often a problem area for writers and editors. Read almost any newspaper or book and you will see that even experienced editors can be confused.

Which introduces a *non-defining clause*. A *non-defining clause* contains additional information that you could omit from the sentence. A comma must be placed before the word *which* and a comma or period at the end of the clause:

> *The car, which a teenager was driving, crashed into a post.*

In this case, the main information is that the car crashed. Incidentally, the driver was a teenager.

That introduces a *defining clause*. A *defining clause* identifies a particular situation, person or object and is essential to the meaning of the sentence. Commas are not used:

> *The car that the teenager was driving crashed into a post.*

In this case, the main information includes the fact that the car was driven by a teenager. Here are some more examples:

Non-defining clause:

> *The bicycle, which she received for her birthday, was too big for her.*

(The focus of this sentence is that the bicycle was too big for her. The additional information is that she received it for her birthday.)

Defining clause:

> *The bicycle that she received for her birthday was too big for her.*

(The focus here is on the birthday disappointment.)

Wrong:

> *The bicycle which she received for her birthday was too big for her.*

Non-defining clause:

> *The telephone, which he tried to use, was broken.*

Defining clause:

> *The telephone that he tried to use was broken.*

Wrong:

> *The telephone which he tried to use was broken.*

Non-defining clause:

> *The paper, which she held, was wet and torn.*

Defining clause:

> *The paper that she held was wet and torn.*

Wrong:

> *The paper which she held was wet and torn.*

Of course, there are many other uses for *which* that do not require commas. For example:

> *She asked which cup she should use.*

In this case *which* does not start a clause, so there is no comma.

Also there are many other ways in which *that* can be used, as in:

> *Where has my idiot roommate taken that computer?*

Or:

> *Where is that pen?*

If you are not sure whether to use *that* or *which*, try the sentence both ways. If both sound acceptable, then use *that*.

short is beautiful
avoid long sentences

Nothing is more likely to discourage a reader than a rambling sentence or paragraph that appears as a big slab of gray on a page. Our "short and simple" rule applies to words, sentences, phrases and paragraphs.

So what do we do when we have a long, clumsy sentence that just does not work? Simple—we turn it into two or three shorter sentences.

Consider this sentence:

> *Firefighters last night rescued an elderly woman from the first floor of a blazing house, which caught fire when the woman knocked over a kerosene heater while trying to get to the telephone in the dark.*

Nothing is grammatically wrong with this sentence, but it is trying to express far too many ideas at once. Better to write:

> *Firefighters rescued an elderly woman from the first floor of a blazing house last night. The house caught fire when the woman knocked over a kerosene heater. The woman tripped in the dark while trying to reach the telephone.*

Another example:

> *The council has given $1 million to build a swimming center, which will have a main pool, a lap pool and*

massage facilities as well as special facilities for the disabled.

Better to write:

The council has given $1 million to build a swimming center with special facilities for the disabled. The center will have a main pool, a lap pool and massage facilities.

Or consider this:

American households now save only eight cents of every dollar they earn after tax, a fraction of the rate at which their parents saved a generation ago, and raising concerns about the country's economic future.

Again, the writer is trying to express too many ideas in one sentence. A professional editor might rewrite it like this:

American households now save only eight cents of every dollar they earn after tax. This is a fraction of the rate at which their parents saved a generation ago. This reduction in savings has raised concerns about the country's economic future.

Another example:

Police are searching for the driver of a white, late-model car with possible damage to the front after a hit-and-run driver killed a cyclist on Market Street early this morning.

Better to write:

Police are searching for a hit-and-run driver who killed a cyclist on Market Street early this morning. Police said the white, late-model car might have damage to the front.

As you can see, it is easier to understand two or three short sentences than one sentence with too many words and ideas. A skilled editor will make sure sentences are short, active and snappy.

briefly speaking
a guide to shorter, simpler words

A key to clean, clear writing is to use as few words as possible to get your message across. Never say in three words what you can say in two. Never use two words when you can use one. And never use a long word when a shorter word will convey the same message.

We are in the business of communication. We want as many people as possible to understand easily what we are saying. The simpler the message, the easier it is to understand.

Longer words certainly have their place because they often offer different shades of meaning—but never use a long word just to show how clever you are. You are not clever if your reader has difficulty understanding what you have written or edited. Sometimes, it is even preferable to use two short words instead of one long word if this makes a sentence easier to understand.

Here are some common examples of how fewer and/or shorter words can give your writing that extra zap. (In some contexts, the ho hum versions can be justified, but in most cases your writing will benefit from the extra zap.)

Ho hum	*Extra zap*
a group of 15 people	15 people
a large number of	many
a multitude of	many
a number of	several, some
a number of occasions	several times
a plethora of	many
a raft of	many

Ho hum	*Extra zap*
accommodate	house, hold, contain
accompany	go with
acted as	was
adjacent to	next to
all of	all
alleyway	alley
allows for	allows
altercation	fight, brawl
amidst	amid
amongst	among
appeared on the scene	appeared, arrived
apprehend	catch, arrest, grab, hold
approximately	about
are in agreement	agree
are in dispute	disagree
are in need of	need
as a result of	because of
as from	from
as many as	up to
as to whether	whether
as yet	yet
ascertain	find out
assistance	help
at a faster rate	faster, more quickly
at an early date	soon
at present	now
attempt	try
at that time	then
at the present time	now
at this moment	now, today
at which time	when
bald-headed	bald

Ho hum	*Extra zap*
became aware of	learned, found out
behind schedule	late
benefit	help
beverage	drink
broke down and cried	cried, wept, sobbed
burst into flames	caught fire
call a halt	stop
check out	check
close proximity	near
collision	crash, smash
commence	start, begin
commented	said
conceal	hide
concept	idea
concur	agree
conspicuous by their absence	absent, away, not there
constructed	built
consult with	consult
crashed into	hit
crisis situation	crisis
currently	now
deceased	dead
demonstrate	show
departed	left
despite the fact that	although
dilapidated	run-down
discontinue	stop
discussions	talks
dispatched	sent
donate	give
due to the fact that	because
during the course of	while

Ho hum	*Extra zap*
each and every	each
effect a saving	save
embarked on	started, began
encounter	meet, meeting
end product	result
endeavor	try
erected	built
escalating	growing, rising, increasing
escaped on foot	fled, ran away
establish	found, set up
eventuate	happen, occur
eyewitness	witness
face up to	face
facilitate	ease, help
facility	factory, plant, garage (be specific)
feedback	response
fill up	fill
filled to capacity	full
following	after
for the making of	to make
free of charge	free
gained entrance to	got in, entered
gale-force winds	gale, gales
gave an explanation of	explained
gave chase to	chased
gave consideration to	considered
gave their approval to	approved
general public	public, people
get under way	start, begin
he is a man who	he
head up (an organization)	head, lead
high-ranking	senior

Ho hum	*Extra zap*
hold a dialogue with	talk to
hold an investigation	investigate, probe
hold negotiations with	talk to, negotiate with
hopeful that	hope, hoped
human beings	humans, people
identical	the same
imprisoned	jailed
in addition	also
in attendance	here, there
in excess of	more than
in my opinion	I think
in order to	to
in possession of	has, had
in short supply	scarce
in spite of	despite
in the direction of	toward
in the first instance	first
in the near future	soon
in the process of planning	planning, moving, building
in the course of	while, during
in the wake of	after
in view of the fact that	since, because
incarcerated	jailed
inebriated	drunk
inform	tell
initial	first
initiate	start
innovative	new
inoperative	not working
inquire, enquire	ask
inside of	inside
instruct	teach, show

Ho hum	Extra zap
intoxicated	drunk
is capable of	can
is of the opinion	believes, thinks
join together	join
laid to rest	buried
large amount of	lots of, plenty of, much
large number of	many
leaving much to be desired	unsatisfactory, poor
lengthy	long
less expensive	cheaper
locate	find
located at	at
location	place
made a contribution	gave, donated, contributed
made a decision	decided
made an apology	apologized
made an approach to	approached
made his way	went
made redundant	sacked
made their escape	escaped, fled, ran away
made their exit	left
made the ruling	ruled
made use of	used
major breakthrough	breakthrough
majority of	most
manufacture	make
massive	huge, big
maximize	boost, increase
meet up with	meet
meet with	meet
members of the public	people, public
merchandise	goods

Ho hum	*Extra zap*
methods	ways
module	part, unit
moreover	also
necessitate	require
necessity	need
non-professional	amateur
numerous	many
objective	aim, goal
obtain	get
occurred	happened, took place
on account of	because
on a daily basis	daily
on one occasion	once
one man, woman	a man, woman
one of the (students)	a (student)
one third	a third
outside of (the house)	outside
owing to the fact that	because
parameters	limits, guidelines
participate	take part
pathways	paths
per annum	a year
per hour	an hour
per week	a week
permit	let, allow
personnel	workers, staff
placed under arrest	arrested
posed a question	asked
possessed	had
preparatory to	before
presently	soon
prior to	before

Ho hum	Extra zap
proceeded to leave	left
proliferation	growth
provide	give
provide extra money for	boost funding
provided that	if
purchase	buy
pursue (someone)	chase
raze to the ground	raze
reason why	why
reduce	cut
reimburse	repay, refund
relating to	about
relocate	move
remuneration	pay, salary, wages
render assistance	help
rendered unconscious	knocked out
repair	fix
request	ask
requires	needs
residence	house, flat
rest up	rest
retail outlets	shops
retain	keep
right here	here
roadways	roads
sat down	sat
seek employment	look for work
short distance away	near, close
situated at	at
situated close to	close to, near
spectrum	range
spotted	saw

Ho hum	*Extra zap*
start	upstart
state-of-the-art	latest
stated	said
stood up	stood
strike action	strike
submitted his resignation	resigned, quit
subsequently	later
substantial	big
suffered a broken leg	broke his, her leg
sufficient	enough
sum of $5000	$5000
take action on	act on
take into consideration	consider
take into custody	arrest
terminate	end, finish, stop
tighten up	tighten
transmit s	end
try out	try
until such time as	until
utilize	use
virtually	almost
was in the process of	was
were required to	had to
whilst	while
witnessed	saw
woke up	woke, awoke
worst-case scenario	at worst

pronouns
how to avoid confusion

A pronoun is any word that stands in place of a noun. *He, she, it, they, their, them, his, her, it, its, my, mine, you* and *your* are pronouns. They are used in sentences in the following ways:

Lucy is absent because she is sick.

The students are lazy. They never do their homework.

She forgot her book. It is still at home.

The dog wagged its tail.

Pronouns can cause problems for even the most experienced writer. At best, a misplaced pronoun can mislead or confuse the reader. At worst, a misplaced pronoun can make nonsense of what you have written.

Consider this:

The students left their books at the park. They were too busy playing tennis.

Now this is nonsense because the plural pronoun they refers to the last plural noun, *books*. So the sentence tells us that the books were too busy playing tennis. Really?

Or:

> *The cat waited patiently beside its food bowl. It was*
> *hungry.*

The singular pronoun *it* refers to the last singular noun, the *food bowl*. So we are saying that the food bowl was hungry. Have you ever seen a hungry food bowl?

Consider this:

> *Detective John Jones had Bill Jackson jailed because he*
> *wanted revenge.*

Who wanted revenge, the detective or Bill Jackson? What the writer means is the detective wanted revenge. But that is not what the sentence says. The pronoun he refers to the last noun that precedes it—in this case Bill Jackson.

So how do we get over this problem? Simple—instead of using the pronoun, repeat the noun. The sentence then reads:

> *Detective John Jones had Bill Jackson jailed because*
> *Detective Jones wanted revenge.*

It is now clear who wanted revenge. Or we could write:

> *Detective Jones, out for revenge, jailed Bill Jackson.*

In the earlier examples, we would make things clear by writing:

> *The students left their books at the park. The students*
> *were too busy playing tennis.*

Or:

> *The students were so busy playing tennis they left their books at the park.*

And:

> *The cat waited patiently beside its food bowl. The cat was hungry.*

Or:

> *The hungry cat waited patiently beside its food bowl.*

Another example:

> *The teacher looked at his student coldly. His lips were curled in a sneer.*

Whose lips? The context indicates that the teacher is sneering. But the pronoun *his* refers to the last noun, the student. We solve the problem by repeating the teacher. We then have:

> *The teacher looked at his student coldly. The teacher's lips were curled in a sneer.*

Or:

> *The teacher, his lips curled in a sneer, looked at his student coldly.*

Either way, there is now no ambiguity. The teacher is sneering.

feeling single, seeing plural
more tricky pronouns

A curse upon those pronouns. Look at this familiar sentence:

> *It is important for a person to know their rights.*

Indeed it is important. But if there is only one person, why are we using the plural possessive *their*? And to whose rights are we referring—the person in the sentence or, say, three other people?

This unusual situation arises because the English language—despite its remarkable adaptive qualities and flexibility—does not deal with this circumstance.

Certainly we may link singular subjects with plural possessive pronouns when we speak, but spoken and written English are often different. So, what to do? Well, we could make the sentence:

> *It is important for a person to know his rights.*

But this excludes half the population. The same issue arises if we change the sentence to read *her* rights. Who says the person is a female? But we could write, for example:

> *It is important for a person to know his or her rights.*

Or:

> *It is important for a person to know his/her rights.*

Another solution is to use the impersonal *one* (meaning a male or a female). Then we would have:

It is important for one to know one's rights.

But these constructions seem clumsy and stilted. An easier solution exists. In this case we change the word *person* to the plural:

It is important for people to know their rights.

Another example:

An athlete is only as good as their coach.

The same problem applies—we cannot say *his* coach or *her* coach, because we are referring to athletes in general, not specifically males or females. The solution here is almost the same as the previous example. We can write *his or her* or *his/her* or *one's.*

An athlete is only as good as one's coach is ambiguous and reads poorly. A more graceful construction would be:

Athletes are only as good as their coaches.

Here is another example:

The former mayor said the council was incompetent and called on them to resign.

Again, we have one subject (*the council*), but a plural pronoun (*them*). To solve the problem, we could change *them* to *it*, but this reads poorly. We could easily write:

The former mayor said the councilors were incompetent and called on them to resign.

It is usually best not to use plural possessive pronouns to refer to singular nouns/subjects. Remember, there is a way to deal with almost every awkward situation.

collective nouns
which verb form do I use?

A collective noun is a singular word for a group of people, animals or objects. For example:

a class of students

a flock of birds

a herd of cows

Because collective nouns are singular, they take a singular verb. Thus we have:

the audience is

the class is

the club is

the committee is

the crew is

the family is

the fire brigade is

the flock is

the group is

the herd is

the police force is

the team is

Green Bay (football team) is

However, when writing about individuals who make up a group, or when the name of a team, group or club ends with an *s*, we use the plural verb *are*:

> *audience members are*
>
> *the students are*
>
> *club members are*
>
> *committee members are*
>
> *crew members are*
>
> *family members are*
>
> *fire brigade officers are*
>
> *the birds are*
>
> *group members are*
>
> *the cows are*
>
> *the police officers are*
>
> *team members are*
>
> *Baltimore players are*
>
> *Green Bay players are*
>
> *the Baltimore Orioles are*
>
> *the Green Bay Packers are*

Collective nouns offer plenty of room for debate and variation.

For example, the word *couple* (as in man and wife). *Couple* certainly is a collective noun. Therefore we technically should write:

The couple is going to different classes.

A couple was rescued after its car went over a cliff.

But this can sound awkward and sometimes plain silly (*is, was, its*). The secret is to regard a couple as two entities—and use a regular plural:

The couple are going to different classes.

A couple were rescued after their car went over a cliff.

The same situation applies to the word *family*. We can regard a family as one unit (collective noun) or as a number of people (plural).

clichés
avoid them like the plague

A cliché is a tired, overused phrase, adjective or expression that people have used so often it no longer has any meaning or has become a vague term that disguises a lack of facts. For example, *speculation was rife* tells us nothing. For all we know, the writer has invented the speculation or rumor. Here are some clichés:

acid test

alive and well

at the end of the day

back to square one

be taken to the cleaners

beat around the bush

between a rock and a hard place

blushing bride

bolt out of the blue

bury the hatchet

burning issue

busy as a bee

by the book

call it a day

consummate professional

do or die

easy as pie

fairytale wedding

get down to brass tacks

give the green light to

going/moving forward

grasping at straws

green with envy

guts and determination

hit the nail on the head

iconic

in the final analysis

in the right ball park

key driver

know the score

last but not least

last-ditch stand

make or break

miracle baby/mom/birth

monotonous regularity

move the goalposts

name of the game

no-brainer

outside the box /square

paragon of virtue

part and parcel

perfect storm

push the envelope

raft/suite (of changes/legislation/etc.)

red-letter day

rest upon one's laurels

rise to the occasion

sadder but wiser

shock the nation

singing from the same hymn book

sink or swim

skating on thin ice

stand the test of time

survival of the fittest

take no prisoners

tears of joy

throw in the towel

to all intents and purposes

trials and tribulations

tried and true

tropical paradise

variety is the spice of life

winter wonderland

writing on the wall

A skilled writer does not use clichés. Unless, of course, the writer is mocking the use of clichés, as in the heading for this section.

the future that is to come
the tautology trap

The future that is to come is a tautology, that is, it says the same thing twice. We know the future is to come—that is what *the future* means. There is no need to say it is to come.

Another example is *looking back to the past*. If we are looking back, it must be the past—there is no need to say it.

Here are some other tautologies:

10 a.m. in the morning—a.m. tells us it is in the morning

4 p.m. in the afternoon—p.m. tells us it is in the afternoon

added bonus—a bonus is something added

ATM machine—the "m" stands for "machine" (automated teller machine)

blue in color—blue tells us it is a color

descend down—to descend is to go down

final outcome—an outcome is final

four acres of land—acres tells us it is land

invited guest—a guest is someone invited

new innovation—an innovation is new

past history—history is in the past

PIN number —the "n" stands for "number" (personal identification number)

remanded in custody—remanded means in custody

return back—to return is to go back

rise up—to rise is to go up

safe haven—a haven is safe

temporary reprieve—a reprieve is temporary

true facts—facts are true

stating the obvious
first cousin to the tautology

Do not state the obvious—it is a waste of words, and detracts from the power or impact of a sentence or headline rather than adding to it. Consider this headline:

Thirty die in bus tragedy

Clearly it is a tragedy—there is no need to tell the reader. In fact, we must always treat the word *tragedy* with care. Even one person, let alone 30, dying in an accident is a tragedy. Better to write:

Thirty die in bus crash

Or consider this:

A huge fire destroyed a $100 million chemical plant outside Newfield last night.

A fire that destroys a $100 million chemical plant is hardly a small fire—so why say *huge*?

Here are some common examples of tautologies and stating the obvious:

abolish altogether	abolish
absolute truth	truth
brand new	new
complete monopoly	monopoly
equally as good as	as good as
first became	became
first found	found

first learned	learned
four-day period	four days
future plans	plans
future potential	potential
future prospects	prospects
grateful thanks	thanks
he himself	he
I myself	I
I personally	I
in actual fact	in fact
lonely hermit	hermit
mental anguish	anguish
mutual cooperation	cooperation
old adage	adage
patently obvious	obvious
planning ahead	planning
pre-arranged	arranged
pre-booked	booked
pre-planned	planned
pre-ordered	ordered
razed to the ground	razed
serious danger	danger
set a new record	set a record
seven different countries	seven countries
severe devastation	devastation
sworn affidavit	affidavit
timber plank	plank
total blackout	blackout
total population	population
totally full	full
totally empty	empty
visibly upset	upset

there, there
a few little words we can do without

Whenever a sentence starts with *there were/there are/there was*, your alarm bell should go off again. In most cases, these words are not needed. Consider the following:

> *There were six chairs in the room.*
>
> *There were eight people on the bus.*
>
> *There was only one other person in the cinema.*
>
> *There are at least 20 plates in the sink.*
>
> *There was a big, dirty rug on the floor.*
>
> *There are at least 30 jobs to be done.*
>
> *There are more than 15 people still to arrive.*
>
> *There were only a few cakes left.*

These sentences should read:

> *Six chairs were in the room.*
>
> *Eight people were on the bus.*
>
> *Only one other person was in the cinema.*
>
> *At least 20 plates are in the sink.*
>
> *A big, dirty rug was on the floor.*
>
> *At least 30 jobs need to be done.*
>
> *More than 15 people are still to arrive.*
>
> *Only a few cakes were left.*

The sentences without *there were/there are/there was* are shorter and have more energy.

Remember, we are putting the odds on your side. Keep things short, snappy and accurate—your editor will love you.

putting on the style
be consistent

Copy can be written in many ways, none of which might actually be wrong. Styles can vary widely between publications. For example:

- Do we write *Sergeant-Major* Bill Jones, *Sergeant Major* Bill Jones, *Sgt.-Major* Bill Jones or *Sgt.-Maj.* Bill Jones?
- Do we write *100 miles an hour, 100 mp/h* or *100 mph*?
- Do we write *inquire* or *enquire*?
- Do we write the *Reverend* Fred Black or the *Rev.* Fred Black? And, after first mention, is he still the *Reverend* or does he become *Mr.*?
- Is someone an *adviser* or an *advisor*? A *vendor* or a *vender*?
- Do we make a *judgment* or a *judgement*?
- Do we allow use of partial sentences in some situations?

There is nothing wrong with any of these, but each publication would have a particular style for each example. Editors and writers for these publications learn the house style. Some of the style choices that work well in this book—such as use of partial sentences and beginning sentences with *And* or *But*—would violate the styles of some other publications.

Newspaper and magazine publishers often use styles generally based on the *Associated Press Stylebook*. Book publishers often base their styles loosely on The *Chicago Manual of Style*. For digital content, the *Yahoo! Style Guide* is often considered standard. For freelance writers, it is a good idea to read a publication to determine its style preferences before submitting any material.

The secret for all writers is to be consistent. When writing and editing your own copy, or editing someone else's, make sure you say the *same thing the same way* throughout. This makes for a cleaner, clearer, professional manuscript.

Here are some basic rules that are standard for many (but not all) publications.

- *Spell out* numbers under 10, for example, *seven*. For 10 and above, use figures. Make an exception with approximate numbers: *"In a thousand or more years."*

- A percentage sign looks too much like what it is—a mathematics symbol—so spell it out. Write *five percent* or *25 percent*, *not* 5% or 25%. In another variation, some publications prefer to spell *per cent* as two words.

- *Do not* use a comma in four-digit numbers, for example, *1824*. Numbers of five or more digits take a comma—*10,809* or *100,307*

- Avoid abbreviations. In your text, write *Camberwell Road* and *Pitt Street*, not *Camberwell Rd.* and *Pitt St.*

- *Never* use the two-letter postal abbreviations for states *(AL, CA, NY, MT)* unless you are giving a full postal address. Otherwise, if you must abbreviate, use the older standard forms *(Ala., Calif., N.Y., Mont.)*.

- *Use* honorifics *(Mr., Ms., Mrs., Miss, Dr.)* after the first mention of someone's name. For example, if we say *Rebecca Jones* on first mention, after this she is *Ms. Jones* or *Mrs. Jones*. She is not *Rebecca*. Or she may then become simply *Jones*, a common style choice these days.

- An exception is sometimes made in references to children in feature stories. In some publications, children's full names are used on first reference, then their first names only.

- Formal titles, when placed before the person's name, take a capital letter: *President Lincoln, Managing Director Allison White.* When used descriptively, such titles are placed after the name in lower case: *Lincoln, who was president . . . Allison White, the general manager . . . .*

- Avoid using acronyms or contractions of initials unless they are universally known, or better known by the initials than by their full names. If you are referring casually to the *Printing and Kindred Industries Union*, write out the full name at least on first reference, and consider just calling it *the union* after that, unless its members universally know it as *PKIU*.

- As always, there are plenty of exceptions to keep us on our toes. Because we know certain institutions so well by their shortened names, it is acceptable to use *IBM, FBI, UN, AFL-CIO, IMF, UNESCO* and *NATO*.

When in doubt, remember the most important rule is to be consistent.

punctuation
basic rules

The apostrophe

The apostrophe shows we have omitted one or more letters and shortened two words into one—a contraction. Some common examples are:

can't—cannot

couldn't—could not

didn't—did not

doesn't—does not

don't—do not

hasn't—has not

haven't—have not

won't—will not

isn't—is not

it's—it is

shan't—shall not

shouldn't—should not

wasn't—was not

wouldn't—would not

The possessive apostrophe

The possessive apostrophe indicates ownership or that one thing belongs to another. For example:

> *Betty's shoe does not fit. (The shoe belongs to Betty.)*
>
> *Somebody's books are on the floor. (The books belong to somebody.)*
>
> *The woman's coat is stylish. (The coat belongs to the woman.)*

Singular possessive nouns take apostrophe *s* (*'s*) at the end of the word. Plural nouns already ending in *s* take only an apostrophe. Here are some examples of singular and plural possessives:

Singular	*Plural*
the car's tires	the cars' tires
the blouse's buttons	the blouses' buttons
the cat's milk	the cats' milk
the student's books	the students' books
the truck's windows	the trucks' windows

Sheep and *deer* are exceptions because the singular and plural are the same. For the possessive plural we add an *s* and put the apostrophe after the *s*.

Singular	*Plural*
the deer's antlers	the deers' antlers
the sheep's wool	the sheeps' wool
The cannon's barrel	the cannons' barrels

But what if a singular noun already ends in an *s*? Traditionally, you would add an apostrophe plus an *s*. But many newer and less formal style guides say to add just an apostrophe. Choose your style and stick to it. For example:

Charles' or Charles's wallet

James' or James's belt

Mr. Harris' or Mr. Harris's shirt

the princess' or the princess's gown

The choice is the same even when the final *s* in the singular noun is not pronounced.

Descartes' theorem or Descartes's theorem

What about plurals of nouns that already end in an *s*? Again, there are two ways to show the possessive. You could use the ownership noun (*Harris*, in the example below) as an adjective, and use no apostrophe because *Harris* is descriptive. Or, you could add *es*, then an apostrophe, because that construction is possessive. Thus we have:

the Harris party or the Harrises' party

the Jones house or the Joneses' house

the Rogers horses or the Rogerses' horses

The plurals of certain common nouns do not end in *s*. The changed spelling tells us the words are plurals. In these cases the singular possessive applies—add an apostrophe, then an *s*. Plural nouns to which this rule applies are *children* (child), *men* (man), *people* (person) and *women* (woman). Thus we have:

the children's coats

the men's coats

the people's choice

the women's coats

There is one exception to the rule that possessive nouns and pronouns should carry an apostrophe. When the word *it* becomes a possessive pronoun, there is no apostrophe. Thus we have:

The house was red. Its roof was green.

The blouse was blue. Its collar was yellow.

The only time the word *its* has an apostrophe is as a contraction of *it is*, in which case the word becomes *it's*:

It's hot today.

It's no good.

And herein lies the problem—if we made the singular *it* possessive with an apostrophe the result would be the same as the contraction—*it's*. And if we were to put the apostrophe after the *s* (*its'*), we would have a plural possessive for a singular pronoun. So we solve the problem by dropping the possessive apostrophe.

Apostrophes occur in some holidays and other special observances:

Mother's Day (a day belonging to mother)

Father's Day (a day belonging to father)

New Year's Eve (the eve belonging to the new year)

But:

Presidents' Day (honoring more than one former president)

Quotation marks

When using direct quotes, remember that the comma or period goes inside the closing quote mark. Thus we have:

"I'm so hungry I could eat a horse, but I'll wait for breakfast," she said.

In the U.S., the same rule applies even when using a second direct quotation within direct quotation marks:

> *"He was angry. He said to me, 'I can't do the job,' and then he hung up."*

Or:

> *"She was very happy. She said to me, 'I've never had such a beautiful present.'"*

Putting all three quote marks at the end of the sentence above looks awkward even though it is standard in most U.S. styles. Usually there is no need for quotations within quotations, so the issue can be avoided. We can make the sentence easier to read by paraphrasing the second quotation. Thus we would have:

> *"He was angry. He told me he couldn't do the job and then he hung up."*

Or:

> *"She was very happy. She told me she had never had such a beautiful present."*

For quotation marks in headlines, the common style is to use only single quotes. For example:

> *Athlete 'back from the dead'*

Or:

> *'I was afraid to tell the truth'*

But as widespread as these style choices may be, individual publishers may vary from them in their own style books. There is no right or wrong about this—just different styles.

Commas

Let us continue our walk through the punctuation minefield into the land of the comma.

Just where do commas go? They certainly cause confusion when a person's title and name occur together. In this case, there are two ways to deal with the situation, both correct. Again, it is a matter of style.

One version takes two commas, the other takes none. The clue is this—a definite or indefinite article (*the, a, an*) is the trigger for commas. Thus we have:

> *The managing director, Brenda Johnson, told shareholders yesterday . . .*

> *An independent candidate, Bob Bloggs, said today . . .*

> *A company spokesman, Jack Spratt, said last night . . .*

Without the definite or indefinite article, these would become:

> *Managing Director Brenda Johnson told shareholders yesterday . . .*

> *Independent candidate Bob Bloggs said today . . .*

> *Company spokesman Jack Spratt said last night . . .*

Commas also separate items on a list. But should there be a comma before the word *and* at the end of a list? Styles differ. Here are two variations:

> *Please bring your new tablet, your smart phone and at least one harmonica.*

Or:

> *Please bring your new tablet, your smart phone, and at least one harmonica.*

Some styles leave the comma off when it does not affect the meaning, but add it when needed for clarity. For example:

> *For the picnic, Mary made ham, tuna, peanut butter, and egg sandwiches.*

Without the comma, some of those sandwiches may have had both peanut butter and egg. With a comma, we know there were peanut butter sandwiches and egg sandwiches.

None of these variations is inherently incorrect. As always, pick the style that seems best to you or follow the style of the publisher you are writing for.

Hyphens

We no longer hyphenate some words. For instance, *black board began* life as two words, then became *black-board* and finally *blackboard*.

So it is with words such as *newsletter, checklist, lifestyle, townhouse, feedback* and *girlfriend*. Some words appear to be still in transition. Whether you write *child-care* or *childcare* depends on the style you are using.

The hyphen is important for clarity, meaning and accuracy. The hyphen shows us that two or more words, or two parts of one word, belong together.

Here is an example of the difference the placement of a hyphen can make:

> *She is a short-story writer.*

> *She is a short story-writer.*

You see the difference. Is she a person who writes short stories, or is she a story writer who is only three feet tall?

The hyphen should be used:

- in adjectival phrases and compound adjectives—the *three-story* house, a *last-minute* change, a *well-educated* woman, an *up-to-the-minute* presentation, a *down-to-earth* person. However, adjectival phrases containing an *-ly* adverb do not take a hyphen. So we would write: a *newly cut* lawn, the *freshly painted* house, a *swiftly flowing* stream, a *poorly designed* house.

- in some compound nouns (which vary in different style books)—*hat-trick, passer-by*—or compound verbs—*cross-examine, hand-pick.*

- to avoid confusion when a word can have two meanings, such as *re-formed* and *reformed.*

- to separate two vowels when we pronounce each vowel differently, such as *re-enter.*

But, I repeat: be consistent.

Colons

We use colons mainly to introduce lists, explanations, examples or formal quotations.

Thus we have:

> *The meatloaf should contain the following ingredients:*
>
>> *2 lbs. hamburger*
>> *2 onions*
>> *2 carrots*
>> *1 garlic clove*
>> *salt and pepper to taste*

And:

> *Lord Nelson reputedly said before the Battle of Trafalgar: "England expects that every man will do his duty."*

And:

> *He loved six things in the world: wine, women and song and more wine, women and song.*

In the last example, many publications that use less formal styles might prefer a dash:

He loved six things in the world—wine, women and song and more wine, women and song.

For examples, see how colons and dashes are used throughout this book.

Semicolons

Be careful how you use semicolons in general text. They can create a sentence that is clumsy and too long. Use a period instead, then write another sentence.

The best use for semicolons is to separate a series of items when each item already contains commas. For example, the result of a horse race might show the winner's name, the jockey's name and the trainer's name. The second-and-third place winners would follow the same format. Thus we might have:

Race four (1200m): 1. Golden Glow, Jim Hockley, Bill Jones; 2. Royal Slipper, Arnold Mell, Alan Spale; 3. Bright Moon, Martin Bole, Rhys Tinwald.

Exclamation marks

With rare exceptions, do not use them. They add nothing. In fact, they often detract from the impact of a phrase or sentence.

Periods and abbreviations

Periods go at the end of a sentence and at the end of some abbreviations.

Acronyms and contractions based on initials such as *NATO, FBI*, and *AARP* usually use no period. *U.S.* has periods because the letters otherwise would spell the word *us*. (Some style books, however, have more complex rules for this.)

Proper nouns and titles that start with a capital followed by lower-case letters (Mr., Mrs., St., Rd., Ave., Sgt., Rev., Gen.) require periods.

Parentheses and brackets

Parentheses enclose a word, clause or sentence that is not grammatically essential to the text, but which adds information or qualification. For example:

She cherished her necklace (a black opal on a silver chain) because Joe had given it to her.

When do you use brackets instead of parentheses? The most common instance is inside a quotation, for explanatory material that is not part of the actual quote:

"I liked the video he put up on his [Facebook] page," she said.

In other words, she did not say "Facebook" but we added it to clarify her meaning for our readers.

contractions
when, and when not, to use them

Don't is a contraction of *do not, won't* is a contraction of *will not, can't* is a contraction of *cannot* and *shouldn't* is a contraction of *should not*. We are talking about turning two words into one.

So when do we use a contraction and when do we use the full words? After all, both are correct. A good rule of thumb is this: do not use contractions unless you are writing direct speech. For example:

> *"I don't care what Mrs. Smith thinks about the closing time," Mr. Jackson said.*

In indirect speech this becomes:

> *Mr. Jackson said he did not* (not *didn't*) *care what Mrs. Smith thought about the closing time.*

Or:

> *"I couldn't go last night," she said.*

Becomes:

> *She said she could not* (not *couldn't*) *go last night.*

Contractions in indirect speech and body text (and in headlines and captions) make the text seem casual and even lazy.

A casual approach may be okay if you are writing a personal blog or e-mail letters mainly your friends will read. This is because you are writing personally, more like the way you talk.

But in other writing, play it safe.

to quote or not to quote
direct and indirect speech

When editing or writing for newspapers, magazines or newsletters, it is important not to use too much direct speech at once. It can be boring to read and boring to look at on a page.

So how do we make things more interesting? The secret is to swing back and forth between direct and indirect speech. This is a basic journalistic technique you will see in newspapers every day.

Consider this extract of direct speech from an interview with Bill Green:

> *"I think we need to ban fishing in the lake for the next three years to give stock a chance to replenish. There are just too many people fishing and not enough fish and the anglers have been ignoring the ban on fishing between May and September.*
>
> *"It is high time the council took some action, or we will soon have a lake with no fish in it at all. Really, a few selfish anglers are spoiling things for the others who respect the rules.*
>
> *"I intend to take up the matter at the next meeting of the council."*

Mr. Green is rambling on a bit here. So how do we make him sound more interesting? To add more action and interest, we turn Mr. Green's direct quotes into direct and indirect speech. Then we have:

Bill Green said fishing in the lake needed banning for three years to give stock a chance to replenish. He said a few selfish anglers, who ignored the fishing ban between May and September, were spoiling things for other anglers.

"It is high time the council took some action, or we will soon have a lake with no fish in it at all," he said. Mr. Green said he would raise the matter at the next council meeting.

While Mr. Green's speech may have been interesting to those who heard it, your written report is made more readable by alternating direct and indirect speech.

tricky, tricky
serial or cereal?

Anyone who finds this book worth reading might pay the author a *complement*—or should that be *compliment*?

Here are some common pairs of words that people often spell or use wrongly:

accede	**agree**
exceed	surpass
accept	**receive**
except	excluding
aid	**help**
aide	assistant
among	**more than two involved**
between	two involved
ascent	**rise**
assent	consent
bazaar	**marketplace**
bizarre	strange, grotesque
because	**due to**
since	from a time earlier
cereal	**edible grain, breakfast food**
serial	story broadcast or published in installments
cite	**to quote as an example**
sight	vision
site	position or place

coarse	**rough in texture**
course	unit of study, golf course, part of a meal
complement	**to complete**
compliment	to praise
continual	**repeated**
continuous	uninterrupted
councilor	**local council member**
counselor	person who counsels or advises
debutant	**male**
debutante	female
dependant	**noun**
dependent	adjective
desert	**lots of sand, abandon**
dessert	sweet course of a meal
desperate	**reckless from despair**
disparate	unrelated
discreet	**wise, judicious**
discrete	detached from others, separate, distinct
disinterested	**impartial**
uninterested	apathetic
dual	**double**
duel	armed contest between two people
effect	**noun, or rarely a verb meaning to create**
affect	verb, or rarely a noun meaning an emotional state
fewer	**numbers**
less	amount
fiancé	**male**
fiancée	female

illicit	**illegal**
elicit	to draw out facts, information, a response or reaction
immanent	**inherent**
imminent	soon to happen
eminent	distinguished
insure	**to arrange for compensation for possible loss or damage**
ensure	to make certain or safe
its	**possessive form of it**
it's	contraction of *it is*
mooted	**suggested, proposed**
muted	muffled, silenced
past	**noun or adjective**
passed	verb
principal	**main, head of school**
principle	rule or moral guideline
prostate	**male gland**
prostrate	face down
stationary	**not moving**
stationery	writing materials
their	**possessive form of they**
there	adverb, showing location
they're	contraction of *they are*
whose	**possessive**
who's	contraction of *who is*
your	**possessive form of you**
you're	contraction of *you are*

the plurals trap
don't get caught

Plurals can cause problems, especially with nouns that end with *o* (*hero*) or *ey* (*monkey*), and with Latin-based and French-based nouns that keep their original plurals. Watch out for these:

Singular	*Plural*
addendum	addenda
attorney general	attorneys general
beau	beaux or beaus
bureau	bureaux or bureaus
cactus	cacti or cactuses
calculus	calculi or calculuses
consortium	consortia or consortiums
criterion	criteria
cupful	cupfuls
curriculum	curricula or curriculums
datum	data
die	dice
fish	fish or fishes
fungus	fungi
hero	heroes
index (math)	indices

index (of a book)	indexes
louse	lice
medium (newspaper)	media
medium (psychic)	mediums
memorandum	memoranda or memorandums
minimum	minimums
monkey	monkeys
nucleus	nuclei
octopus	octopuses
person	people (not persons)
phenomenon	phenomena
plateau	plateaus or plateaux
potato	potatoes
sister-in-law	sisters-in-law
spectrum	spectra or spectrums
spoonful	spoonfuls
squid	squid or squids
stadium	stadiums
tomato	tomatoes
valley	valleys

One simple rule to remember: for nouns ending in *ey* (*monkey*), simply add an *s* (*monkeys*). For nouns ending in *y* (*folly*), change the *y* to *i* and add *es* (*follies*).

under a spell
a handy guide to difficult words

Writers regularly spell certain common words wrongly. Even editors sometimes miss errors in such words as:

accessible

accommodation

all right

argument

barrel

berserk

buoy

cappuccino

colossal

commit

committee

condescending

connoisseur

conscience

conscientious

definitely

desperate

diarrhea

dilemma

disastrous

discern

dissatisfaction

eighth

embarrass

exhilaration

existence

feasible

gauge

grammar

hemorrhage

hemorrhoids

harass

hindrance

hygiene

irresistible

liaison

miscellaneous

mischievous

necessary

occasion

occur

occurrence

outrageous

pastime

parallel

perseverance

personnel

persuade

precede

prestigious

privilege

proceed

pursuit

questionnaire

recommend

reminiscence

renown

restaurateur

resuscitate

rhyme

rhythm

sacrilegious

seize

separate

sergeant

siege

supersede

unconscious

woolen

oops

the misplaced phrase

A phrase or clause in the wrong place can make nonsense of a sentence. Consider this:

> *For the sixth time this year, a pedestrian has been injured on South Road.*

Surely not the same pedestrian.

Or:

> *The committee discussed building a car park in the council chamber.*

A small car park or a big chamber?

Or:

> *She owned a mixing bowl designed to please a cook with a round bottom.*

Mixed up indeed. Yet the situation is easily solved just by moving certain words around:

> *A sixth pedestrian has been injured on South Road this year.*
>
> *The committee discussed in the council chamber whether to build a car park.*
>
> *She owned a mixing bowl with a round bottom, designed to please a cook.*

Always check for sense what you have written or edited.

if only

be careful to say what you mean

Here we have another small, seemingly innocent word that can cause plenty of problems. If only writers and editors would take more care when they use the word *only*. The placement (or misplacement) of *only* (usually an *adverb*—a *how* word) can cause confusion by changing the meaning of a sentence.

The most common misplacement of *only* is this:

She only had three lemons left.

The reader could think this means:

She alone has three lemons left.

But what the writer means is:

She had only three lemons left.

Or in other words:

Three lemons were all she had left.

Another example:

He struggled on because he only had two miles to go.

The reader could think this means:

He alone had two miles to go.

But what the writer means is:

He struggled on, because he had only two miles to go.

Or in other words:

Two more miles and he would reach his destination.

The secret is to place the word *only* as close as possible to the word or phrase you wish to emphasize. In the examples above the *only* is meant to refer to *the three lemons* and *two miles*, so we place the word *only* as close as possible to these words.

Here are six more sentences that show how the placement of only can change the meaning:

She only dreamed of becoming manager of Briggs Ltd.

(She did nothing about it.)

Only she dreamed of becoming manager of Briggs Ltd.

(No-one else was interested.)

She dreamed of becoming only the manager of Briggs Ltd.

(She did not want to become the chief executive officer.)

She dreamed only of becoming manager of Briggs Ltd.

(She dreamed of nothing else.)

She dreamed of becoming the only manager of Briggs Ltd.

(She was not interested in sharing the job.)

She dreamed of becoming the manager of Briggs Ltd. only.

(She had no interest in managing any other company.)

Take great care that the position of *only* in your sentences does not create ambiguity or give the wrong meaning.

now, see here
look out for this common error

Most common nouns cannot see anything—yet some writers insist that these nouns have developed eyes. For example:

February saw a change in the government's tactics.

February cannot see anything. February does not have eyes. What the writer means is:

The government changed tactics in February.

Or:

In February, the government changed tactics.

Another example:

Next year will see the start of work on the new freeway.

A year cannot see anything. A year does not have eyes. What the writer means is:

Work will start on the new freeway next year.

And finally:

The shooting saw the start of an all-out gang war.

Again, a shooting cannot see anything. The writer means:

The shooting triggered an all-out gang war.

So keep your eyes open for this common error—and fix it.

kid stuff
avoid slang

We all use slang when we speak:

> *I dropped the kids off at school.*

> *Get your gear off the floor.*

> *Would you like a cuppa tea?*

But when writing and editing, avoid slang in all text except direct speech. Slang is sloppy, so write:

> *children not kids*

> *clothes not gear*

> *cup of not cuppa*

> *bicycle not bike*

> *friends not pals or buddies*

> *alcohol not booze*

former, latter, last
how to keep order

Another little minefield is the use (or misuse) of the words *former* and *latter*. Former and latter apply to two people or objects. For example:

> *Carol White and Jane Black are friends. The former (Carol White) lives in Los Angeles, the latter (Jane Black) lives in New York.*

If there are three people, the third would be the *last*, not the *latter*.

> *Carol White, Jane Black and Jill Green are friends. The former (Carol White) lives in Los Angeles, Jane Black lives in New York and the last (Jill Green) lives in Denver.*

get to the point

how to write a news story

The introduction

The first paragraph, or *introduction*, is the most vital part of any piece of writing. This introduction:

- must sum up clearly what you want to say.
- must tell the reader what your story is about.
- must get to the heart of the matter.
- is the bait, or the hook, to grab the reader's interest.

When writing an introduction, remember the *who, what, where, when* principle. For example:

> *Four students (who) found $1 million (what) on a New York subway car (where) yesterday (when).*

In many cases, it is a good idea to add the *how*. For example:

> *Four students found $1 million on a New York subway car yesterday when they searched under their seat for a dropped iPhone.*

The introduction tells the reader what the news story is about, in slightly more detail than is possible in the headline, while revealing its most interesting angle. Without this information, the reader will see no reason to read the rest of the article.

Therefore, skilled editors and writers will make sure they do not bury the introduction in the fourth or the seventh paragraph.

When writing or editing a news story, always ask yourself: what is the most interesting angle? What is the point that will grab the reader or sum up what this article is about? Then write your introduction clearly and in the active voice.

For a news story, the introduction should be no longer than 30 words. If there is no way to meet that limitation, be sure to break it into two or more sentences. Do not be afraid to rewrite the introduction as many times as you need.

The good news is that once you get the introduction right, you will be surprised how easily the rest falls into place.

The body

The second part of a story, the *body*, should expand on the introduction. The body should explain in more detail what the story is about. It should contain facts and quotes that build on the introduction and add depth, explanation and substantiation.

The information should be presented in order of importance.

The tail

The final paragraphs are known as the *tail*. The tail contains the least important details. It should not matter if the tail is cut for space reasons. A well-written news story can easily be cut from the bottom.

The standard style for writing a news article is often referred to as an "inverted pyramid." Its foundation is at the top, followed by material that is less and less essential.

heads, you win

how to write a headline

Writing headlines is a specialist occupation. Newspaper and magazine editors learn this particular (and complex) skill over many years. For anyone writing headlines, whether for a newspaper, magazine, brochure or newsletter, here are a few basic tips:

- Headlines should contain a verb. A verb makes a headline active. For example:

  Widow celebrates lottery win

  Volunteers save rare ducks

  Voters turned away

- An understood verb can be acceptable. The understood verb (*is* or *are*) does not appear. For example:

  Driver (is) not to blame

  Missing toddlers (are) home again

  Our roads (are) a health hazard

- Avoid label headlines. Headlines without a verb are dull and tell us nothing. For example:

  Town hall meeting

  Missing boy

  Council report

Rather than being dull labels, the headlines should tell us what happened at the meeting, that people are searching for the missing boy, and that the council is broke. Then we might have:

Mayor shouted down at meeting

200 search for missing boy

Council bankrupt, report warns

Much more interesting, surely?

- Remember that cute little passive voice word *by*? Well, do not use it in headlines—it is a killer.

- Avoid definite (*the*) and indefinite (*a, an*) articles. They slow things down. For example:

Woman sues council over land

is much preferable to:

A woman sues council over land.

- Most headlines are in the lower case, except for the upper case letter at the start and for a proper name. There are exceptions, though. For example, the *New York Times* does not follow this rule.

- Avoid acronyms and initialisms except for those that are universally known among your readers, such as USA, NATO or FBI.

- Do not put a period at the end of a headline.

- Be wary of using names of people or places that may be unknown to some readers.

- It is a good idea to set headlines left, not centered.

- In a two-line headline, the top line should be longer than the bottom line, and the bottom line should be at least three-quarters the length of the top line. This is easy on the eyes.

- Three-line headlines should not be out of balance, with the words getting longer and longer, such as:

  Council
  newsletter
  proves popular

  A more-balanced shape would be:

  Newsletter
  proves
  big success

  Another acceptable shape would be:

  Council
  newsletter
  popular

- Headlines should be in the present tense, even when the event happened in the past. For example, the President might have warned yesterday that America was in for tough times, but the headline might read:

  President warns of tough times

  Or:

  Tough times ahead, President warns

- Double-check that your headline makes sense and that it does not have two meanings. Otherwise you could end up with headlines like these (real examples):

  Dead pilot flew without license

  Children make tasty biscuits

  Miners refuse to work after death

  Stolen violin found by tree

  Or the famous headline from World War II:

  Eisenhower flies back to front

editing checklist
a last round-up

You have completed your written material (news or feature article, report, business presentation, Web page, blog, whatever it is) or have it before you to edit. So what comes next? Before you get down to the nitty-gritty of fine-tuning the material, carry out the following steps:

1. Check that the text begins with the brightest, most interesting *introduction* or *angle*. Make sure you have not buried your introduction in the body of the article.

2. Check *punctuation*. Make sure periods, commas, apostrophes, dashes and quotation marks are correct.

3. Check that all words that should have *capital letters* have them. Likewise, check for words that have capital letters but should not have them.

4. Check the *spelling of names*. Make sure you spell names the same way throughout the text and in captions. Likewise, check the spelling of street and place names.

5. Check all *spelling and grammar*. Remember to use your spellchecker *and* your eyes *and* a dictionary.

6. Check the text for *style*. If it is your own material, make sure you use a consistent style. If you are editing

the material for a specific publication, make sure the copy is in the style of that publication.

7. Check the text for *passive voice*. Change to active voice when possible.

8. Make sure your *sentences* are short and clear. Remove jargon, clichés and tautologies. Simplify complex phrases. If you can use one word instead of two, do so. If you can use a short word instead of a long word, do so.

9. Make sure *paragraphs* are not too long.

10. Make sure you attribute all *quotations* and *allegations* to someone.

11. Check that the text does not *defame* anyone or breach *copyright*. If in doubt, get a legal opinion.

12. If you need to edit the text to a specific *length*, cut the copy as required. If the copy is well written, you should be able to cut from the bottom. It is also often possible to delete less-important quotes.

13. When you are satisfied you have edited the copy to the highest standard, *read* it again—first for sense, then for spelling and grammatical errors.

hot tips

things to remember

1. *Refute* means to prove wrong. *Rebut* means to deny or argue against.

2. *Prostate* is a male reproductive gland. *Prostrate* means face down.

3. *Compare to* means to liken one thing to another. *Compare with* notes similarities and differences.

4. You are different *from me*, not *than me.*

5. *Fewer than* is for numbers. *Less than* is for quantities.

6. One cupful, two cupfuls. One phenomenon, two phenomena.

7. Use adverbs sparingly.

8. Avoid exclamation marks.

9. When you write the word *that,* try reading the sentence aloud without the word.

10. When either *which* or *that* sound right in a sentence, *that* is almost always correct.

11. Do not be afraid to repeat a noun to make your meaning clear.

12. Decades written using numerals—*the 1970s*—do not have an apostrophe. If you shorten it to *the '70s,* an apostrophe is needed to replace *19.*

13. If a sentence is too long, turn it into two—or even three—sentences.

14. Two-word adjectives should be hyphenated—*hydrogen-filled blimp*—unless the first of the words ends with *ly*—*terribly dangerous blimp.*

15. *Who* is the subject, *whom* is the object. *Who does what to whom?*

and finally

set your standards high

"But hang on a minute," you might well say. "Every time I pick up a newspaper or a magazine I find all the things this book tells me not to do. What's going on?"

Sadly, you are right. You will see passive voice in introductions (*the man was hit by the car*), stating the obvious in headlines (*30 die in bus tragedy*), clichés (*gave the green light to*) and contractions in indirect speech (*he said he didn't know how it happened*).

You will also find spelling errors, place names spelled wrongly, split infinitives, names spelled differently in captions and text, typographical errors and confusing pronouns.

Our aim is to do better than this. As writers and copy editors of our own text or someone else's, our mission is to ensure that all aspects of the text are correct. Set your standards high.

And good luck.

resources
things to keep handy

If you do a lot of writing, you will need resources at your fingertips.

The internet is a starting point—often you can quickly double-check facts, spelling and grammar quickly online.

If you are writing a personal blog, the ability to make intelligent searches may be all you need. But do not assume accuracy unless you know and trust the source.

Books (paper or digital) that many good writers and editors keep at hand include:

- At least one good dictionary of American English, such as the *New Oxford American Dictionary* (Oxford University Press, USA) and/or the *American Heritage Dictionary of the English Language* (Houghton Mifflin Harcourt). These are more complete and authoritative than the free online dictionaries. Language changes rapidly, so invest in editions that have been updated most recently.

- A modern thesaurus. In practice, not all writers like using a thesaurus, but if you do, good ones include *Roget's Super Thesaurus* (Writers Digest Books) and *Oxford American Writer's Thesaurus* (Oxford University Press, USA). Many others exist, and their usefulness is subjective, so it is worthwhile to browse.

- If most of your writing is in a specific subject area, a specialized dictionary for that niche.

- If you are writing books, *The Chicago Manual of Style* (University of Chicago).

- If you are writing for newspapers or magazines, the *Associated Press Stylebook* (Perseus Books).

- If you mainly write material for the Web, The *Yahoo! Style Guide* (Yahoo!).

- If you are writing or editing term papers and academic or business reports, the *Publication Manual of the American Psychological Association* (APA Books).

- *Elements of Style* by William Strunk and E. B. White (Macmillan). Although some advice in this short book is outdated, most of it is timeless. This quick, easy read has inspired generations of writers.

Most serious writers have several reference books, or even a shelf full of them. Keep an eye on good bookstores and/or Web stores for new editions of the books that will help you the most.

index